Thoughts and Feelings

Thoughts *and* Feelings

Please

Written by Ruth Shannon Odor
Photos by David M. Budd

The Child's World®, Inc.

Published by The Child's World®, Inc.

Copyright © 2000 by The Child's World®, Inc.
All rights reserved. No part of this book may be
reproduced or utilized in any form or by any means
without written permission from the publisher.
Printed in the United States of America.

Design and Production:
The Creative Spark, San Juan Capistrano, CA

Photos: © 1998 David M. Budd Photography

Library of Congress Cataloging-in-Publication Data

Odor, Ruth Shannon, 1926–
     Please / by Ruth Shannon Odor.
          p. cm.—(Thoughts and feelings)
     Summary: Simple rhyming text describes the importance of saying,
"Please" and being polite.
     ISBN 1-56766-672-8 (lib. bdg. : alk. paper)
     1. Etiquette for children and teenagers. [1. Etiquette.]   I. Title. II. Series.
BJ1857.C5036   1999
395.1'22—dc21   99-25377
                                                                              CIP

There's a special word that begins with a "P."

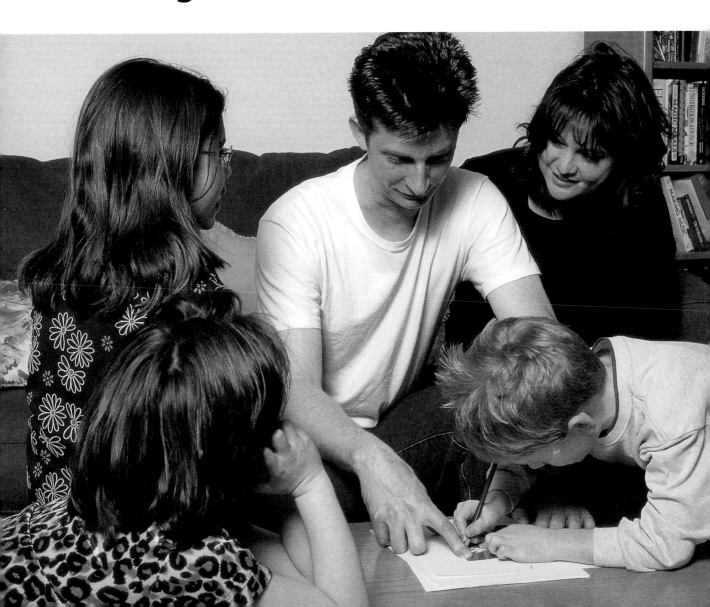

It's a very big part of good
manners, you see.
It's a word to say often
when talking to others,
to teachers, friends, parents,
to sisters or brothers.

It's one of two "magic" words that some people say. Polite people use it several times a day.

Have you guessed my riddle, as quick as a breeze? Then you know that the answer is the word,

"PL

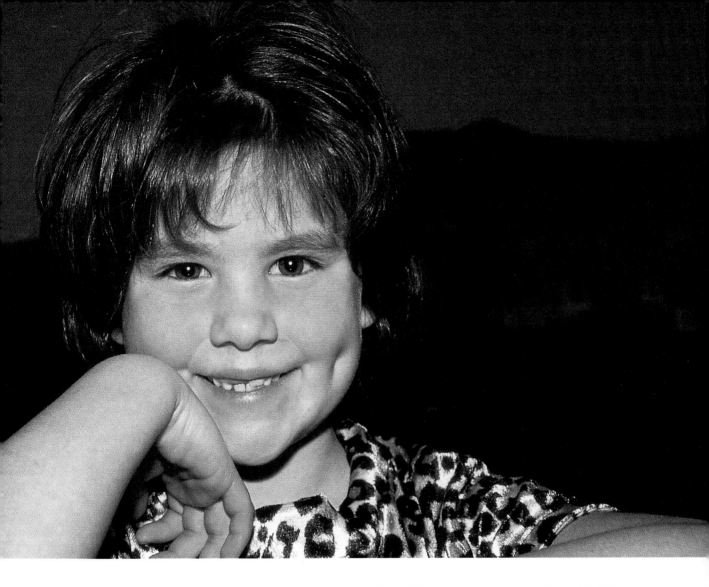

It's better to say,
"Please pass the bread,"

than to reach across the table...

and fall
on one's head.

You'll find that your father often agrees whenever you use the magic word, "Please."

When you want a favor
from a sister
or brother,

18

use the word, "Please."
It will work
like no other.

"Please, may I play with your frisbee? The one that is blue?"

With a smile sister Kelsey
will hand it to you.

At school, always say,
"Please, it's my turn."

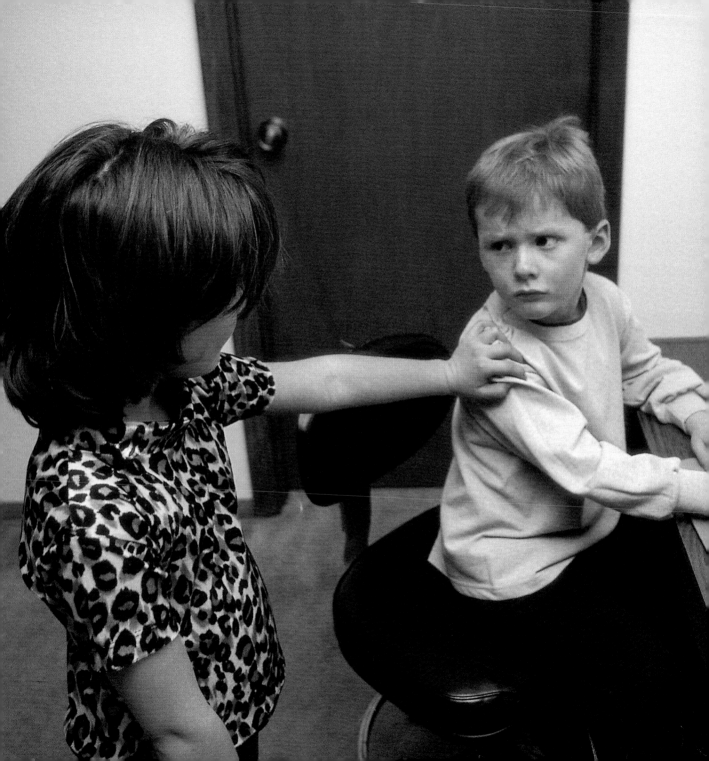

Don't push or shove.
This is important
to learn.

The teacher is happy
whenever she sees
a child who remembers
to say the word, "Please."

On the phone, I say, "May I please speak to Chad?"

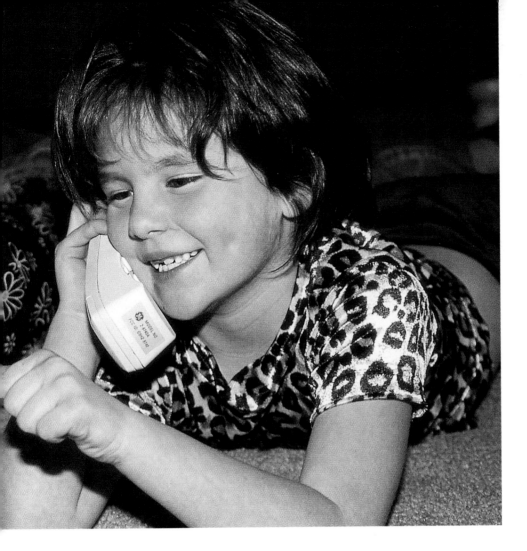

"Just a minute, I'll get him,"
answers his dad.

Saying please is being kind
and considerate, too.
It makes people glad to
be around you.

And just as I'm glad I
learned the "ABCs"
I'm glad that I learned to
say the word, "Please."

For Further Information and Reading

Books

McGrath, Bob. *Oops! Excuse Me Please! And Other Mannerly Tales.* Hauppauge, NY: Barron's Juveniles, 1998.

Scarry, Richard. *Richard Scarry's Please and Thank You Book.* New York: Random House, 1973.

Vail, Rachel. *Please, Please, Please.* New York: Scholastic Trade, 1998.

Ziegler, Sandra. *The Child's World® of Manners.* Chanhassen, MN: The Child's World, 1998.

Web Sites

Learn a fun outdoor activity that reminds you to be polite: http://family.go.com/Features/family_0401_01/dony/donyout_group/donyout191.html

Top seven manners kids should know: http://www.lifetimetv.com/parenting/kidman.html

For information about thoughts and feelings: http://www.kidshealth.org/kid/feeling/

Fairy tales and stories about thoughts and feelings from all over the world: http://www.familyinternet.com/StoryGrowby/